HIGH DAYS AND HOLIDAYS

High Days and Holidays

A reading-aloud collection

Chosen by Eileen Colwell
Illustrated by Maureen Bradley

VIKING KESTREL

To the many, many children with whom
I have shared and enjoyed stories

VIKING KESTREL
Penguin Books Ltd, Harmondsworth, Middlesex, England
Viking Penguin Inc., 40 West 23rd Street, New York, New York 10010, USA
Penguin Books Australia Ltd, Ringwood, Victoria, Australia
Penguin Books Canada Limited, 2801 John Street, Markham, Ontario, Canada L3R 1]
Penguin Books (NZ) Ltd, 182-190 Wairau Road, Auckland 10, New Zealand

First published 1988

British Library Cataloguing in Publication Data

Highdays and holidays.
  1. Children's literature, English
  I. Colwell, Eileen
  820.8′09282   PZ5

  ISBN 0-670-81928 X

Printed and bound in Great Britain by
Butler & Tanner Ltd, Frome and London

Contents

To Parents

Young children find the everyday world wonderful and exciting. Birthdays, making friends, moving to a new house, holidays by the sea – all are occasions to be enjoyed with enthusiasm.

The stories in this book are about some of the 'high days and holidays' of childhood. Not many children will meet the Queen, of course, but adults will recognize the historic celebration of the Queen's sixtieth birthday, a 'high day' and a holiday for thousands of children.

To hear and read stories is essential for a child's development and in this parents have an important part to play.

Eileen Colwell

J for John

John was very excited for it was his birthday – and, what luck – it was snowing!

He ran downstairs in great excitement. How many presents would he have this time? What would they be?

The table was laid for breakfast and there was a special brown egg for him. He looked eagerly for his pile of presents beside his plate. There were *no* exciting parcels at all, only *one* little box! Whatever had happened?

'Mummy!' he said, almost crying. 'Am I only getting *one* present this year?'

His mother smiled comfortingly. 'Open that box, dear, and see what's inside it,' she said.

John opened it. Inside there were three keys – a big one, a middle-sized one and a very small one. There was a piece of paper, too, and on it was printed a big letter 'J'.

'Is this my present, Mummy?' he asked. He felt very puzzled and disappointed too.

'It's your present from Daddy and me – Granny and the Aunties will give you theirs tonight. Daddy and I thought that as it's such a short time since Christmas and you had lots of presents then, you might like to have your birthday presents in a different kind of way. So we've *hidden* three presents for you. When you find out where these keys fit, you'll find your presents too. Each one will have a big "J for John" tied on to it so that you will know that it is yours.'

'I'll begin looking now,' said John, jumping up from the table.

'Eat your breakfast first,' said his mother.

Breakfast over, John had a good look at the three keys. 'I'll try the middle-sized one first,' he decided. 'It looks the easiest.'

He ran round the house in a great hurry, trying to fit the key in all kinds of locks. Some were too large so that the key almost disappeared in them, others were too small so that the key wouldn't go in at all. He had no luck downstairs, so he went upstairs to his mother's room. He tried the drawer in the dressing-table and the chest of drawers

– no luck. Then he tried the wardrobe – CLICK – the key turned and the door opened.

There were his mother's dresses and her fur coat. John rubbed his face against it, he liked its pussy-softness. But where was his present? He rummaged about and there was a box! Tied to it was a label with a big 'J for John' on it.

He sat down on the floor to open the box. Inside was a pair of wellingtons, real boys' 'wellies'. 'I'll be able to go out in the snow even when it's as deep as deep,' he thought.

Now he chose the small key. It was too small for any *door* in the house, too big for his mother's little bureau. But one of the doors in the sideboard in the dining-room was locked. He fitted the tiny key in the keyhole – CLICK – it turned. Inside, among the table-cloths, was a parcel wrapped in gay paper and tied on to it was a label with a big 'J for John' printed on it.

John tore open the paper. Inside was a very special kind of woollen cap with flaps to go over his ears – just like the one his father had brought back from Canada. He put it on at once. His ears felt warm as toast – it would be fine to wear in the snow.

There was a pair of red woolly gloves in the parcel as well. Now his feet and his ears and his hands would all be warm in the snow.

Now there was only the big key left. He tried it in every lock in the house but it was too big for any of them. 'Wherever does this one fit?' he asked his mother despairingly.

'I mustn't tell you,' she said, 'but I think you've often seen someone using it.'

John sat down by the fire to think. Whoever would use a big key like that? Why, his father of course! 'I know,' he shouted, jumping up. 'It's the key to the shed. I'll go outside and try it.'

'Wrap up warmly first,' said his mother. 'It's still snowing.'

'I shall put on my new wellingtons,' said John busily, 'and my gloves and I've got my cap.'

'Don't forget your anorak!' said his mother.

Soon John was dressed and ready. He opened the door. Brrrr – how cold it was! The lawn was white and smooth except for the little criss-cross marks made by the birds' feet. He put his foot in the snow – it was quite deep. But his father had cleared a path to the garage and the shed.

Big flakes of snow were falling and tickling his nose. He plodded to the shed door and put the big key in the lock. It fitted! He had to use both hands to turn it but – CLICK – it opened the door.

Inside were his father's garden tools and his lawn mower. There was the wheelbarrow – but where was his present?

Suddenly he saw it – a large parcel wrapped in brown paper and, on top of it, a label with a big 'J for John'.

Whatever could be inside the parcel? It was quite long but not very thick. He tore a corner of the paper and peeped inside. He could see something red and made of wood. Could it be –? He stripped off the paper in a hurry – yes, it *was* a sledge, the thing he had wanted more than anything! It was a beauty, too, painted bright blue and red, with shining runners and a thick white cord to pull it by.

What a good thing it was Saturday tomorrow and his father would have a holiday. What fun they would all have!

And so they did, rushing down a hill on the sledge, falling over in the snow and climbing the hill to do it all over again.

It was the most exciting birthday John had ever had!

Vera Colwell

The Hippopotamus's Birthday

He has opened all his parcels but the
   largest and the last;
His hopes are at their highest and his
   heart is beating fast.
O happy Hippopotamus, what lovely gift is
   here?
He cuts the string. The world stands still.
   A pair of boots appear!

O little Hippopotamus, the sorrows of the
   small!
He dropped two tears to mingle with the
   flowing Senegal;
And the 'Thank you' that he uttered was
   the saddest ever heard
In the Senegambian jungle from the mouth
   of beast or bird.

E.V. Rieu

A Friend for Danny

Danny's hamster died a week before the Family Pets' Service at Danny's church.

Danny was very sad about it. He carried the hamster round in a large box that his mother gave him, until it was quite obvious that Lord Birmingham would have to be buried.

'Why?' asked Danny.

('Whiffy!' murmured his sister Jane unkindly.)

'No it isn't!' said Danny stubbornly, but he took the box down to the bottom of the field and buried his hamster in a beautiful grave, with flowers, and put a cross on top covered with silver paper.

'I've buried Lord Birmingham!' he announced, coming in to tea.

'That's lovely!' said his mother, 'Now we'll burn the box, shall we?'

'I want the box!' Danny said. 'I have a new pet in it now. I need the box to keep her in.'

'And what *is* she?' asked the family.

16

'I found her at Lord Birmingham's grave,' Danny said, 'and she told me she would like to come and live with me for ever instead of him. She was sorry for me.'

More than that Danny would not say. He punched holes in the lid of the box, but he held on to it so tightly that nobody could peep inside.

The new pet was very quiet.

After tea Danny took the box into the garden and picked leaves to put inside it. The family watched him.

(Too many leaves for a caterpillar, too few for a rabbit, and five different kinds of leaves too!)

Danny put them all in the box and tied it down with string.

'Could it be a bird?' asked his sister Jane.

'Birds don't eat all those leaves! They eat seeds and crumbs. And water too!' his sister Hazel said.

When Danny left the room for a minute both his sisters tried to peer through the holes, but there was absolutely no way in which they could see anything inside it, and nothing could be heard inside the box at all.

'It's very light!' said Jane, lifting the box.

'I think he's just pretending!' said Hazel.

But Danny came back at that moment, and was so angry with them that it became apparent there was something in the box that he did not want his sisters to see.

'Has it got a name?' they asked him.

'Yes, she's called Queen Victoria!' Danny said shortly, carrying away the box. 'I shall ask the vicar to bless her on Sunday!'

The week went by and the family nearly forgot about the box, which lived underneath Danny's bed. His sisters were very busy practising for their school sports.

'Don't you ever clean it out?' Jane asked him one day.

'Yes, of course I do! But not when you're around!' Danny said sharply.

'And doesn't it mind living down there in the dark?' asked Hazel.

'She likes it!' snapped Danny.

'Oh do let us look at it, please Danny!' begged both his sisters.

'You can see her at the service on Sunday!' Danny said forgivingly, and with that they had to be content.

Sunday came, and everyone brought their pets to church.

Jane took the family dog, while Hazel carried the budgie in a cage. Danny carried his great big box, with all the string taken off it, but as he neared the church he began to feel embarrassed. He dawdled behind his sisters, and on the church steps he accidentally tripped and fell over, in front of everybody.

The lid flew off the box, and Danny sprawled on the ground while a kind lady retrieved it for him. He jammed it on and struggled to his feet, thanking her.

'Wait for me!' he called to his sisters, hurrying up the church aisle to the steps where a whole menagerie of pet animals were waiting to be blessed.

'What's in there, Danny?' the other children were asking. 'What's he got, then?' they pestered his sisters.

Nobody could say.

Danny grew quite red in the face holding the box tightly closed and waiting for the vicar to arrive. He came quite soon.

'And what have you got in that mighty big box?' he questioned Danny.

'It's my pet, and she's called Queen Victoria! Please will you bless her?' said Danny, as all the children pushed and jostled to look inside the box.

'Well, open her up and we'll have a peep!'
said the vicar, and Danny opened the box at
last.

Everybody looked inside. The vicar
looked, Danny's sisters looked, the other
children looked, and Danny looked.

There was absolutely nothing in the box at all.

'There! I knew there wasn't! He's only pretending!' said Jane in disgust.

'Silly twit!' muttered Hazel scornfully.

'I'm not! I wasn't! She *is* there! She is!' cried Danny, searching frantically, but there was nothing to be found, and all the other children were laughing at him.

Danny burst into tears of rage. He flung away the box and charged down the church crying at the top of his voice.

The vicar was about to follow him, but the other children were all waiting with their pets, and it seemed best to go on with the service and maybe to call on Danny afterwards.

They sang the first hymn, and then the vicar began a prayer for all the pet animals and their owners.

Half-way through the prayer there came a piercing shriek from the church porch.

'I've found her! She's here! She's here!'

Up the church, with his hand held high in triumph, marched Danny, and on his outstretched finger rode a lovely little snail.

Fresh from the tumble down the steps she perched on her master's finger with every sign of grace and confidence. Her long horns were extended to notice everything around her ... the tall pillars, the choir stalls, the altar, the pulpit and the vicar.

As elegant as her name she held her head high, and only partly retracted her horns when the vicar touched her gently with his finger.

'This,' said Danny, proudly, 'is my pet snail, Queen Victoria...'

'And now,' the vicar said, a little later on, 'we will say a prayer for Queen Victoria, the little snail belonging to Danny, and a prayer for all God's creatures worshipping here with us today. God bless and keep them all, and their masters and families for ever. For Jesus' sake. Amen.'

Ursula Moray Williams

Snail

Snail upon the wall,
Have you got at all
Anything to tell
About your shell?

Only this, my child –
When the wind is wild,
Or when the sun is hot,
It's all I've got.

John Drinkwater

The Sea and the Sandcastle

Martin was very little. He was only one year old. He could not walk yet, but he could crawl very well indeed. He had a tiny rubber spade and a tiny rubber bucket and he sat, all alone, in the middle of the great big beach.

Every now and then Martin scooped up a little sand on his tiny spade and dropped it over his shoulder. He was trying to make a sandcastle, but he wasn't very good at it. Still, he enjoyed himself a great deal and he chattered away to himself, and to the seagulls who flew over to watch him, and to the far-away sea that whispered at the edge of

25

the beach. 'Swish-swish, swish-swish,' it said.

Presently a little girl came running down the beach. Her name was Nicola.

'Hello, Martin! I'm going to help you,' she called, and began to pile sand on his tiny castle with her wooden spade.

'Na, na, na,' screamed Martin and he waved his spade at her, for he wanted to build his castle in his own way. But Nicola was three and she had come specially to help her little brother, and help him she did. And when Martin saw how well Nicola could build castles he was glad she had come to help him.

They had a very happy time sitting there in the middle of the big empty beach and talking to themselves and each other and the seagulls, and building their little castles. And far away on the edge of the beach, but not quite so far away now, the sea was talking to itself, too. 'Swish-swish, swish-swish,' it whispered.

In a little while another girl came running down the beach. Her name was Alison and she was really quite a big girl, for she was six years old and she went to school.

'Hello, you two, I'm going to help you build a big castle!'

'No, this is our castle, no, no, *no*,' squealed Nicola.

'Na, na, na,' cried Martin.

But Alison was their big sister and she didn't take a bit of notice. She began to dig right away with her iron spade. When Nicola and Martin saw how fast the castle was growing they were glad that Alison had come to help them, and they started to dig again, too.

They all talked to themselves and each

other and had a very happy time. A seagull flew over and cried to his friend the sea: 'They're getting on fast, they're building a castle!'

And, far away, but not so far away as before, the sea whispered and chuckled to itself as it lapped at the edge of the sand. 'Swish-swish, swish-swish,' it laughed to itself.

In a little while quite a big girl came running down the beach. Her name was Hilary and she was the oldest of the family. She had brought her large iron spade with her.

'Hello, you three, I've come to help you build a really big castle!' she shouted.

'No! This is our castle.'

'Na, na, na!'

Alison, Nicola and Martin had been having a very good time together. But Hilary didn't take a bit of notice because she was their big sister. She just started to dig with her big spade and when the others saw how fast their castle was growing now that Hilary was helping them, they were glad she had come. They all dug together as hard as they could, even Martin, though he took as much sand off the castle as he put on it.

The seagull flew over again. 'They're making a very big castle now!' he called to his friend the sea. And the sea, which was much nearer now, whispered and chuckled to itself at the edge of the sand, as it wiped out all the marks that the people had made since last it had washed the beach.

After a while a man came striding down the beach. He carried a great big shovel.

'Oh, Daddy!' laughed the children excitedly, as he began to throw huge shovel-

fuls of sand on top of the castle, all except
Martin, who shrieked, 'Na, na, na,' at the
top of his voice.

The castle grew faster and faster. They all

dug and dug and dug, as hard as they could, even Martin.

Then the seagull flew over again. 'Hurry up, old dear! They're making such a big castle that you'll never be able to wipe it all out if you don't hurry up.'

But this time the sea was very near indeed. It was rather surprised when it saw what an enormous castle the busy family had made. But it didn't worry. It just whispered and chuckled quietly to itself and sent its little waves lap, lapping, towards that castle, nearer, nearer, until, quite suddenly, an extra big wave swished right round the castle.

'No, no, no,' they all cried together. 'Go and wash the beach somewhere else, old sea. This is our castle and we don't want it washed away.'

But the sea didn't take a bit of notice. It was used to people and their castles. It just came swishing in and in, quite gently, wave by wave, until it had made an island of the castle. Daddy had to pick up Martin and take him back to the beach hut. But the sea didn't stop. It came in, further and further, until it got too deep for Nicola and she had to go back to the hut, too.

But still the sea wouldn't stop. In and in it came until, at last, it got too deep for Alison. And then it got too deep for Hilary and she had to go back to the hut. And in the end Daddy found that the sea was splashing his shorts and he had to go in, too.

So there they all sat in the hut, watching the sea coming in and in, and the castle getting smaller and smaller until only the little flag that Daddy had stuck in the top was left above the water and, at last, even that floated away.

'Well, it was a lovely castle,' they all agreed, as they went home to bed. And, next day, when the sea had gone out again, the sand was just as flat as it had been before they began to dig.

The sea was still laughing to itself, far away at the edge of the beach. 'Swish-swish, swish-swish,' it called. 'You can make another castle,' it seemed to say. 'I've made the sand all flat and clean for you to make another one!'

And that's exactly what they did...

Penelope Pine

Sea

Over the hill
first sight of the sea
lying sunlit and still
just waiting for me.

I race from the land
in the clear morning light
to rock pool and sand,
shells whiter than white.

Birds ride the sky,
the wispy clouds there
soft floating, and I
am walking on air.

Leonard Clark

The New Baby

Anna was feeling very cross; her mother had just told her she was going to have a baby soon.

'But we don't want a new baby!' Anna told her. 'You've got me!'

'But darling,' Mummy had said, 'I thought you'd love to have a little brother or a sister. Daddy was sure you would be pleased.'

'Well, I'm not,' retorted Anna, and grabbing an orange from the fruit-bowl, she rushed out to the bottom of the garden and sulked.

She sat on the garden bench and swung her legs which were too short to reach the ground. She did everything she could think of with the orange. She squeezed it hard, stuck her thumb into the skin and sucked out all the juice, shooting out the pips one by one from between her teeth as far as she could, then stuck a small twig in the lawn to mark the place of the longest shot. Next she

35

flung the orange peel high up into the apple tree. She was feeling *very* cross.

She wished she could be riding Jewel, her favourite pony at Mr Barrett's stables, but Mummy was too busy to take her, for she was getting a little cot ready for the new baby and washing the woolly shawl she, Anna, had worn as a baby.

Her mother and father seemed very excited and happy about the new baby and expected her to feel the same. Well, she didn't!

David, her friend next door, had two brothers and a sister, and they all played happily together, but they felt sorry for Anna because she was an only child.

'Don't you wish you had a brother or a sister?' David asked her, but Anna said she liked being the only one.

'My Daddy takes me to watch ponies and horses – and I can ride all by myself!' she said. 'Who wants a baby around the house?'

'Oh, they're fun,' laughed David as he ran off to help his little sister to open the garden gate.

Anna wandered indoors. Her mother was sitting by the window. Anna thought how pretty she looked as she put down her sewing and smiled.

'Hullo, darling,' she said. 'How about going for a run on your new bicycle? I'll come and watch you, shall I?'

'Will I have to let the new baby ride my cycle?' asked Anna jealously.

'Only if you want to,' smiled her mother,

'but you know the baby boy or girl will be far too tiny to do anything like that for a long time. Perhaps you could spare one of your soft toys? Babies love them.'

'Perhaps,' said Anna reluctantly.

Just then they heard a car coming up the drive and Anna rushed to the window.

'Oh Mummy, it's Daddy! Why is he back so soon?'

'When you were down in the garden he phoned to say he would be home soon. He's going to take you to the stables because he has to see Mr Barrett about something,' Mummy told her.

'Oh good-oh! Good-oh!' Anna shouted and ran out to hug her father.

'Daddy, is it true? Are we going to Mr Barrett's? Can I ride Jewel?'

Her father laughed. 'Why, Anna, what a lot of questions! Jump into the car, we're going to the stables right now.' So Anna waved goodbye to her mother who was watching from the window.

Anna and her father chatted happily as they drove to the farm stables. Mr Barrett was unsaddling one of the horses as they drove up and parked the car.

'Hello Anna. Hello Mr Selkirk – I'm glad you've got here in time. Come with me – I've got something to show you.'

'Can I ride Jewel, Mr Barrett?'

'Not today, Anna, but come to her stable, she has a lovely surprise for you.'

'Jewel, a surprise?' Anna exclaimed. 'Oh, what can it be? Come on, let's run!'

So the three of them – Mr Barrett, Anna and her father – raced each other to Jewel's stable.

'Now, quietly, quietly,' Mr Barrett said, putting his finger on his lips. 'We mustn't frighten her,' and opening the stable door carefully, he let Anna go in first.

Anna could hardly believe her eyes. There was her beloved pony Jewel, lying on a bed of straw, and beside her was a baby foal. Jewel was licking her baby very tenderly and her beautiful eyes were full of love.

'Born just ten minutes ago, Mr Selkirk. You asked me to phone you.'

Anna's father nodded. 'Thank you Mr Barrett. I left my office as soon as you called. I *so* wanted to bring Anna.'

Anna was kneeling beside the baby foal and talking to Jewel. She was so thrilled and happy, then looking up at the two men standing by, she said, 'We're going to have a new baby too, aren't we, Daddy. Isn't that exciting, Mr Barrett?'

'It is indeed Anna, and when your baby brother or sister is old enough, Jewel's baby will be ready too, but of course *you* will always ride Jewel.'

When Anna and her father got home, Anna rushed into the house to tell her mother all about Jewel's foal, and then she ran next door to tell her friend David and the other children. 'We're going to have a new baby too, isn't that exciting?'

'Lucky Anna! I told you it's fun to have brothers and sisters,' laughed David. 'Come on, let's all go down the garden to play.'

A few weeks later Anna's father took her to the hospital bed where Mummy was sitting up smiling happily and, cradled in her arms, was the new baby fast asleep.

Anna kissed her mother and looked at the tiny baby's face. So this was her new brother, and she suddenly felt very proud when the baby opened his blue eyes and looked at her.

'May I hold him, Mummy, do you think?'

'Of course, darling.'

So her father lifted Anna on to the bed and very, very gently the baby was put into her arms.

'He's lovely, Mummy. What shall we call him?'

'How about James?' suggested Mummy.

'Oh yes, yes, I like that name. Jewel's baby foal is called Beauty. Oh, I'm so excited. It's very nice to have a baby brother after all!' And after she had kissed the baby and her mother, Anna couldn't get home quickly enough to run and tell her friend David all about her new brother, Jamie!

Judith Garratt

My Brother

My brother's worth about two cents,
As far as I can see.
I simply cannot understand
Why they should want a 'he'.

He spends a good part of his day
Asleep inside the crib,
And when he eats, he has to wear
A stupid baby bib.

He cannot walk and cannot talk
And cannot throw a ball.
In fact he can't do anything –
He's just no fun at all.

It would have been more sensible,
As far as I can see,
Instead of getting one like him
To get one just like me.

Marci Ridlon McGill

The Picnic Basket

One cool summer morning Andrewshek's Auntie Katushka said, 'Andrewshek, I think I will put some sandwiches and some cottage cheese and some poppy seed cakes and two eggs in our picnic basket. Then we will go to the park and eat our lunch there, near the water.'

'May I go with you, Auntie Katushka?' asked Andrewshek.

'Of course you may go to the park with me,' said Auntie Katushka. 'But first we have a great many things to do, before we can go to the park. I must go into the garden and catch the white goat. I will tie her up so she will not run away. Please find the kitten, Andrewshek, and put her in the cellar, so she will not worry the chickens while we are gone.'

'Yes, indeed, I will find the kitten and put her in the cellar,' said Andrewshek, 'so she will not worry the chickens while we are gone.'

44

But all Andrewshek really did was to lift up the red and white napkin which Auntie Katushka had laid over the picnic basket and look at the eggs and the poppy seed cakes and touch the sandwiches and taste the cottage cheese.

The goat was not easy to catch. The goat

wanted to go to the park, too. She galloped round and round the garden.

At last Auntie Katushka caught her and tied her firmly to the post.

Then Auntie Katushka went into the house to get Andrewshek and the lunch basket. She saw Andrewshek peeping under the red and white napkin and tasting the cottage cheese. He had forgotten all about the kitten.

The kitten was nowhere to be found. 'I think she must be paying a visit to the Mouse family,' said Auntie Katushka.

Auntie Katushka put on her bright shawl and took her umbrella with the long crooked handle under one arm. Then she picked up the lunch basket with the red and white napkin on top and she and Andrewshek started for the park.

They went down the hill and across the railway line and past the market and down a long street until they came to the park by the water.

Andrewshek sat down on the grass beside a little stream. Andrewshek's Auntie

Katushka laid her umbrella with the long crooked handle and the basket of lunch on the grass beside Andrewshek.

'Andrewshek,' said Auntie Katushka, 'I must go to the spring and get some water for us to drink. Please watch the basket with the eggs and the sandwiches and poppy seed cakes and cottage cheese while I am gone.'

'Yes, indeed, I will watch the basket of lunch,' said Andrewshek.

But what Andrewshek really did was to say to himself, 'I would like to take off my shoes and stockings and paddle in the little stream. I believe I will.'

Andrewshek took off his shoes and stockings and went paddling in the little stream.

A big white swan came floating calmly down the stream. He saw the basket lying on the grass. He stopped and stretched and stretched his long neck until he could touch the basket. 'Honk! Honk!' said he. 'I wonder what is under the red and white napkin?'

The big white swan lifted the napkin with his red bill and looked in the basket. 'Oh, oh,

oh! Won't Mother Swan be pleased with this
nice lunch!' said he. 'Sandwich bread makes
fine food for baby swans.'

He picked up the basket in his strong red
bill and floated it ahead of him down the
stream.

Andrewshek could not wade after the big swan. The water was too deep.

'Stop! Stop! White Swan!' cried Andrewshek. 'That is my Auntie Katushka's picnic basket and it has our lunch in it. Please put it back on the grass.'

'No, indeed! I will not put the basket back,' honked the big white swan. 'Sandwich bread makes fine food for baby swans and I have ten baby swans to feed.'

The big white swan gave the picnic basket a little push with his red bill. The basket floated on down the little stream. The big white swan floated calmly behind it.

Just then Andrewshek's Auntie Katushka came hurrying up with the spring water. She saw the big white swan floating down the stream with the lunch basket floating ahead of him.

Andrewshek stood in the middle of the stream crying.

Auntie Katushka picked up her umbrella with the long crooked handle. Auntie Katushka ran along the bank until she overtook the big white swan, with the lunch basket floating ahead of him.

She caught the handle of the picnic basket in the crook of her long-handled umbrella. She drew the basket safely to the bank.

'Well! Well!' said Auntie Katushka, as she spread the red and white napkin on the grass, and laid the sandwiches and the poppy seed cakes, and the cottage cheese and the eggs upon it. 'It always pays to carry an umbrella to a picnic!'

Margery Clark

The Friendly Cinnamon Bun

Shining in his stickiness and glistening
   with honey,
Safe amongst his sisters and his brothers
   on a tray,
With raisin eyes that looked at me as I put
   down my money,
There smiled a friendly cinnamon bun, and
   this I heard him say:

'It's a lovely, lovely morning, and the
   world's a lovely place;
I know it's going to be a lovely day.
I know we're going to be good friends; I like
   your honest face;
Together we might go a long, long way.'

The baker's girl rang up the sale, 'I'll wrap
   your bun,' said she.
'Oh, no, you needn't bother,' I replied.
I smiled back at that cinnamon bun, and
   ate him, one two three,
And walked out with his
   friendliness inside.

Russell Hoban

Luke's Exciting Day

Luke woke and sat up. It was his first day at school – at last.

Quickly, he put on his new school clothes. His shirt buttons were stiff to do up and the green jumper felt very long. He tried to knot his tie. 'Over once and over twice,' he muttered. 'Up through the middle and down through the knot.' But it didn't work. The knot wouldn't slide up. So he left the tie on his bed and, quickly opening his bedroom door, he crept downstairs to play with his Lego.

A long time later Luke heard his parents' bedroom door open.

'Luke!' said his mother, coming down the stairs. 'It's only six o'clock.'

'We mustn't be late,' Luke explained.

'Oh well,' said his mother, putting on the kettle. 'At least we won't be rushed.'

When the voice on the radio said, 'The time is half-past eight,' Luke and his father set off for school.

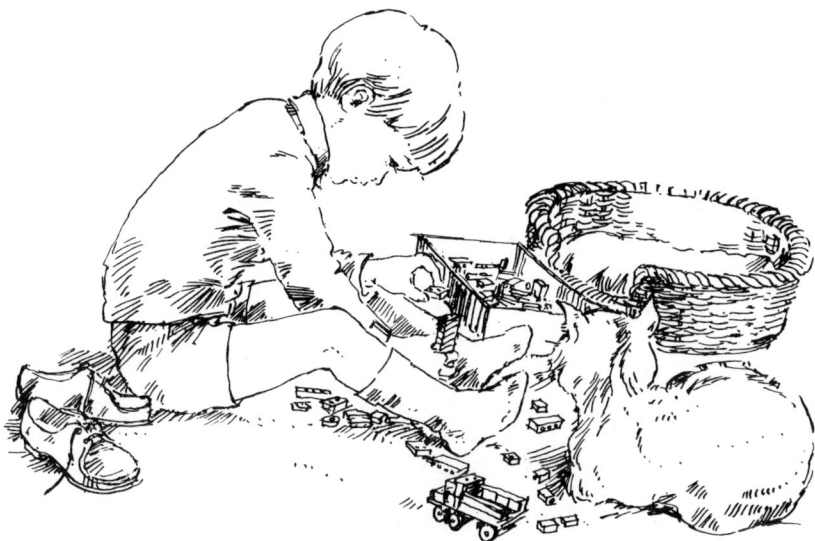

His mother said, 'Be good and enjoy
yourself. I'll see you at half-past three. All
right?'

Luke nodded.

'Your dinner money's in your satchel,
remember,' she added and kissed him. 'You
do look smart. Especially the tie.'

'Daddy did it. Goodbye,' said Luke. He
slung his new satchel over his shoulder and
walked down the road with his father.

When they reached the school there were
lots of other children arriving. Luke looked
around for his friends from the playgroup.

Three of them were starting today, but he couldn't see them yet.

Suddenly his father said, 'Look. Mrs Armstrong has opened your classroom door. We can go in.'

Luke kept hold of his father's hand and together they walked into the classroom. And there was Sarah from the playgroup, holding her mother's hand. She looked a bit strange in her grey pleated skirt. She usually wore dungarees.

'Good morning, Luke,' said Mrs Armstrong. 'Come and see your peg. It has your name above it and a picture of a wheelbarrow to help you remember it. You hang up your coat and satchel here.'

Luke hung up his coat. 'I want to go to the loo,' he told his father.

'Surely not yet!' said his father, but Mrs Armstrong said, 'That's very sensible of you, Luke. Joe wants to go too. So I'll show you both at the same time.'

Near the pegs were two blue doors. 'One is the girls' toilet,' Mrs Armstrong explained. 'And the other is the boys'. Now, you tap on the boys' door and say, "Is there anyone in the boys' toilet?" You do it, Luke.'

'Is there anyone in the boys' toilet?' asked Luke quietly. There was no answer. So Mrs Armstrong pushed open the door and Luke went in. When he came out Mrs Armstrong said, 'Now it's Joe's turn. Luke, you wash your hands in the basin and dry them on a paper towel.'

Luke enjoyed that. He only had ordinary towels at home.

'Now, all of you go and sit down on the carpet in the Book Corner,' Mrs Armstrong called out.

'Then I'll be off,' said Luke's father. 'Tell me all about it this evening.'

Luke hugged his father and ran over to sit by Joe.

Joe looked at him and turned away.

'What's the matter?' Luke asked.

'Nothing,' said Joe. 'It's just the wrong school, that's all. I was going to Carlton School. Then we moved house. I don't know this school.'

Luke sat and thought. 'I came here last

term,' he said. 'I played in the Home Corner. But I don't know it either, really.' And he began to feel sad.

But just then Mrs Armstrong came over to them holding Sarah's hand. 'Here are two sensible boys, Sarah,' she said. 'They'll look after you. Look at a book together.'

Joe knelt up and took a book called *Rumpelstiltskin* out of the rack. 'I've got this one at home,' he said.

'We've got it at our playgroup,' said Sarah.

Soon there were lots of children sitting in the Book Corner and Mrs Armstrong came over to them.

'I think we're all here now,' she said. 'Let's have a rhyme before I mark the register. What shall we sing?'

'The Grand Old Duke of York,' said Luke. And together they all sang, making their hands march up the hill and down again. But Joe didn't sing at all.

'What would you like us to sing, Joe?' said Mrs Armstrong.

'Three little monkeys jumping on a bed,' said Joe.

'Oh? How does that go?' asked Mrs Armstrong.

'I don't know,' said Joe.

'Oh,' said Mrs Armstrong again. 'I'll have to look it up in my book.'

Then Mrs Armstrong showed all the new children their seats at the tables. Luke sat beside Joe. One by one she called out their names from the register and they answered, 'Yes, Mrs Armstrong.'

'Well done,' she said at the end. 'Now I'll give you each a piece of paper and some crayons to do a drawing. Draw whatever you like.'

Luke drew a castle with helicopters flying overhead, and Joe did a monster on top of his new house. Mrs Armstrong wrote some letters on each drawing for the children to copy underneath.

Luke was writing his name on the castle wall when Mrs Armstrong said, 'It's time to play outside.'

Joe went into the playground with Luke. They stood under a tree at the side. Suddenly some big boys arrived and began running round the tree, dodging each other. A little frightened, Joe and Luke moved over to the far corner of the playground. Joe pulled a toy car out of his pocket and they played with that until they heard a whistle blow to tell them it was the end of playtime.

Luke ran back to the classroom door and found the chair he had sat on before play-time. There was a jigsaw on the table in front of him.

'Good. I like jig...' Luke said, turning to Joe's place.

But Joe wasn't there.

Luke found the four corners of his jigsaw and *still* Joe wasn't there.

'Whose is that empty place?' asked Mrs Armstrong.

'Joe's,' said Luke.

'Where can he have got to?' said Mrs Armstrong. She walked over to the coat pegs and called, 'Joe? Are you there?' But there was no answer. 'Hannah, dear,' she said to a bigger girl, 'Can you look out in the playground and see if Joe's there?'

Hannah ran outside. The children could hear her shouting. 'Joe! Joe!' Soon she was back – without Joe.

Luke stood up. 'He said it was the wrong school, Mrs Armstrong. D'you think he's gone to the right school?'

'Oh dear,' said Mrs Armstrong in a

worried voice. 'I must just tell the head-mistress,' and she hurried to the classroom door.

As she opened it – bump! – she walked into Joe.

'Joe!' said Mrs Armstrong. 'Wherever have you been?'

'I went to see the kitchen,' Joe explained. 'There was a lovely smell in the playground. And I followed it. I thought it was sausages. But it wasn't. I went round two corners. The lady there said, "Not long to dinner time." Then she showed me where to come back.'

'Oh,' said Mrs Armstrong. 'Well, that sounds quite an adventure!'

Joe nodded. 'Can I take Luke to see the kitchen now, please?'

'Well,' said Mrs Armstrong. 'I'll tell you what I'll do. I'll ask if we can *all* go and see the kitchen one morning next week. And in the meantime you get on with your jigsaw. All right?'

Joe nodded and sat down next to Luke. 'I'll do yours too, if you like,' he said to Luke. 'I like jigsaws.'

For a while Mrs Armstrong played dominoes with the older children. Luke whispered to Sarah, 'I want to play dominoes too.'

'I want my sandwiches,' said Sarah.

'I haven't got any sandwiches,' said Luke.

'Then you're having school dinners,' said Sarah.

As she said this Mrs Armstrong called, 'Line up if you're having school dinners, children. I'll take you to the hall.'

Luke was very interested to see what they were having. He was very pleased. There were beefburgers and chips, salad and salad cream. The dinner lady gave him some extra tomatoes when he said he liked them.

Joe and Luke ate their dinners and took their plates to the counter to help tidy up. Luke stood behind Joe in the queue. Suddenly he noticed that he had pushed his dirty plate into Joe's back by mistake and Joe's new green jumper had a line of yellow salad cream across it. What should he do? Quick as a flash, Luke darted to the serving

hatch and fetched a wet dish cloth. As Joe
was holding up his bowl for chocolate pudding, Luke rubbed him hard on his back
with the dripping cloth. Joe tipped forward
and – splat – he fell into the huge bowl of
chocolate sauce.

'Sorry!' Luke shouted. 'It was an accident.'

Joe stood up and sauce dripped off the

front of his jumper.

'What did you do that for?' said the poor dinner lady, trying to mop up the mess.

Luke wanted to cry. Then he saw that Joe was laughing. 'I like chocolate sauce,' Joe said. 'I've got it on my nose.'

Mrs Armstrong found Joe an old jumper from the lost property box to wear for the rest of the afternoon. 'Don't worry, Luke,' she said kindly. 'I'll explain what happened to Joe's mother.'

That afternoon the children played outside again. Then they had games in the hall and jumped about to music on a cassette player.

Last of all Mrs Armstrong read them the story of *Rumpelstiltskin* because Sarah wanted it so much.

Towards the end of the story Luke saw his mother walking across the playground. He waved and she put her finger to her lips and smiled.

Mrs Armstrong stood at the door to say goodbye to the children. Joe's mother stepped inside to fetch his jumper.

'Hullo, Mum!' shouted Joe. 'I've got a best friend. He pushed me in the pudding. I didn't mind. I liked it!'

Mrs Armstrong put her hand on Luke's shoulder. 'It was an accident,' she explained. 'But Joe has been very cheerful since dinner time.'

'That's all right,' said Joe's mother, smiling at Luke. 'Joe wanted a friend. You both seem to have had a happy day.'

Luke nodded hard. 'Goodbye, Mrs Armstrong,' he said.

'Goodbye, boys. Be good – if you can,' said Mrs Armstrong.

And all the way home, Luke chattered to his mother about his exciting FIRST DAY AT SCHOOL.

Anne Rooke

Just for Fun: Nonsense Rhymes

Way down South where bananas grow,
A grasshopper stepped on an elephant's
  toe.
The elephant said, with tears in his eyes,
'Pick on somebody of your own size!'

The Crocodile

If you should meet a crocodile,
Don't take a stick and poke him;
Ignore the welcome in his smile,
Be careful not to stroke him,
For as he sleeps upon the Nile,
He thinner gets and thinner;
And whene'er you meet a crocodile
He's ready for his dinner.

66

Little Johnny

Little Johnny fished all day,
Fishes would not come his way.
'Had enough of this,' said he,
'I'll be going home to tea.'

When the fishes saw him go,
Up they came all in a row;
Jumped about and laughed with glee,
Shouting, 'Johnny's gone to tea!'

Ghosts

There were three ghostesses
Sitting on postesses
Eating buttered toastesses
And greasing their fistesses
Right up to their wristesses.
Wcren't they beastesses
To eat such feastesses!

To See the Queen

An almost true story

'Children, something exciting is going to happen,' said the head teacher of a small village school one morning. 'We are all invited to see the Queen!'

'The *Queen!*' exclaimed the children. 'We've never seen the Queen except on telly – and she lives in London.'

The head teacher explained. The Queen was going to have her sixtieth birthday and so thousands of children were going to London to wish her a happy birthday. 'And our school has been chosen to take part in the big procession to Buckingham Palace.'

All the children began to talk at once. How would they get to London? How would they find their way to Buckingham Palace? Would the Queen be able to walk about amongst them as she was so old? Would she wear her crown and jewels?

Mary Bates was the youngest girl in the school. That afternoon when she came home, she hurried to find her mother.

68

'Mummy,' she said excitedly, 'I'm going to see the Queen! I'm going to see the Queen!'

Her parents looked at each other in dismay. 'But, darling,' said her mother, 'you're too young to go all that way and have such a long day.'

'I'm four and a half,' said Mary indignantly. 'The Queen has asked me to go – and she'll miss me if I don't.'

Mary went to bed in tears but in the morning her father said, 'You *may* be able to go to London. I am going to ask your teacher if I can go in the coach to London and help to look after you all. If he will let me, then you can go with me to see the Queen. Mummy is staying at home to look after Baby.'

The weeks before the great day were very busy, for the children had to learn to sing the Queen's birthday song perfectly and some other songs too. They must find out also about the places they would see on the way to London and in London itself. All the children helped to make a big banner with the name of their school and village on it and a big HAPPY BIRTHDAY. The biggest children were going to carry it in the procession.

The great day came at last. Everyone was very early at the school gates to wait for the coach. Their school uniforms were spotless, their faces shone with soap and happiness. Each child carried a packet of sandwiches, for they were sure to be hungry.

The journey was exciting. The children enjoyed watching the traffic on the motor-way and cheering the driver of their coach when he passed other cars. (They would have liked him to speed and pass everyone but he wouldn't.) Soon Mary was asleep for she had been too excited to sleep properly the night before.

Their teacher pointed out the interesting places they passed and when they reached the outskirts of London there was still more to see. Mary woke then. 'Is that Buck'nham Palace?' she asked drowsily when they passed a big building.

'Not long now,' said her father and soon the coach stopped in a large park so that the children could eat their sandwiches – most of them had already eaten them. Now each child was given a bunch of ten daffodils to carry.

Suddenly there were children everywhere, hundreds and hundreds. Boys and girls moved about talking and laughing until their teachers rounded them up and the long procession began to take shape. There were lots of brightly coloured banners – Mary's father read out the names on some of them. Children seemed to have come from all over Britain and from faraway towns too, like Hong Kong and Singapore across the sea. Every child had a bunch of daffodils.

Then the bands played lively marching tunes and the long procession began to move towards Buckingham Palace. So much noise, so many banners – and thousands of yellow daffodils!

In the middle of their school group walked Mary holding her father's hand, for to be amongst so many people was a little frightening – her daffodils clutched firmly in her other hand.

'This wide road is called the Mall,' said her father. 'It leads right up to the Queen's house. We shall soon be there.' But before they got so far, Mary's short legs were tired and she had to have a piggyback.

So, school by school, six thousand children poured into the Queen's front garden (only it didn't look like a garden for there were no flowerbeds). And there, school by school, they gathered behind a railing near to the Queen's front door, so that they could all see the Queen when she came out on to the balcony overhead. Mary's father couldn't stay with her because he was too tall to stand in the front row, but a girl said she would take great care of her and a policeman put her near him where she could hold on to the railing and be sure to see the Queen.

Then the soldiers' bands played and everyone sang jolly songs. 'When can we sing "Happy birf'day"?' asked Mary anxiously.

'WE WANT THE QUEEN!' shouted the children – thousands of children can make a lot of noise! And all of a sudden the doors on the balcony opened and out came ten men dressed in gold with silver trumpets in their hands and blew with all their might. Last of all came a lady dressed in a dress the colour of a daffodil. It was the QUEEN. Mary knew it was, although she wasn't wearing her crown, for she had seen her on the telly.

All the boys and girls cheered and cheered and the bands began to play the special birthday song, 'Happy birthday to you'. And if you have never heard six thousand children sing for the Queen, you have missed something wonderful! And the Queen smiled and smiled and waved her hand like Queens have to.

And at last the Queen came out of her front door to walk amongst the children. Everyone pressed forward waving their daffodils, and in the crush Mary dropped hers and they disappeared underfoot.

Then Mary cried and cried. The girl tried to comfort her but couldn't and someone offered her another bunch of daffodils but she pushed them away.

And then – and then – someone said in a

kind voice, 'What – crying, child, on a birthday!'

'I've lost me flowers,' wailed Mary, 'and now I haven't any to give to the Queen.'

'Well, supposing I give *you* some instead,' said the kind voice and, looking up through her tears, Mary saw the lady in the daffodil dress. It was the Queen herself.

'Thank you, Queen!' said Mary, giving a bob as her mother had taught her, for she knew her manners. And the smiling lady moved on to speak to other children.

Mary remembered little of what happened afterwards – the great courtyard deep in yellow daffodils, the jolly Prince and the pretty lady who held the flowers the Queen couldn't carry. Then the Queen went back on to the balcony and the children sang the birthday song all over again because they *felt* like it. This time Mary didn't join in, she was too tired and, anyway, her father had come to take her home. He carried her all the way to the coach and she fell asleep and didn't wake up until they were safe home again.

'Did you enjoy it, darling?' asked her mother.

'I seen the Queen,' said Mary drowsily. 'An' I didn't have any flowers to give her, so she gave *me* some, she did. I seen the Queen close to . . .' And she fell asleep again.

It was the happiest and most exciting day of her life.

Eileen Colwell

Queen Alice

To the Looking-Glass world it was Alice
  that said
'I've a sceptre in hand, I've a crown on my
  head;
Let the Looking-Glass creatures whatever
  they be
Come and dine with the Red Queen, the
  White Queen, and me!'

Then fill up the glasses as quick as you
  can,
And sprinkle the table with buttons and
  bran:
Put cats in the coffee, and mice in the tea –
And welcome Queen Alice with thirty-
  times-three!'

Lewis Carroll

An Unexpected Visitor

'We'll go to the farm for some eggs this morning,' Grandmother said. 'I'll just sweep up these crumbs first, because of the mice.'

'What mice?' asked Simon. He looked under the table hopefully.

'The mice who'll be popping in if I leave any crumbs about.' Grandmother nodded solemnly. 'You get a lot of unexpected visitors in the country,' she said.

It had been raining hard in the night, and there was thick mud at the farmyard gate. Simon was wearing his new shiny wellingtons.

'Gracious me!' cried Grandmother. 'There's a puddle here as big as a pond!' She gave a mighty leap and landed safely on the other side of it.

'I'll squidge through it,' Simon said. 'My boots will keep me quite dry.'

'Let's hope so,' said Grandmother. 'Now let's go and find Mrs Tippett.'

The farmer and his wife lived in an old

grey stone house that rambled all round the farmyard. It had some green grass in the front garden, with a fence and gate to keep the farm animals out. Mrs Tippett was busy feeding a little cluster of chickens on the lawn. She peered over the top of her spectacles as Grandmother and Simon came up the path.

'Morning,' she said. 'Come for some eggs,

have you? Shan't be a moment.'

'Good morning,' said Grandmother. 'This is my grandson.' She introduced Simon. 'I call him Simpey, but his real name is Simon.'

'Yes,' said Simon, 'and this is my grandmother.'

Mrs Tippett's smile went in and out as though she hadn't meant it to happen. 'Chick-chick-chick,' she said, scattering the last of the hen food.

Simon sat on his heels to get a good view of the chickens eating. 'These are very pecky little things,' he remarked.

Just then a loud mournful noise rose and fell upon the air.

'That sounds like Hilda.' Grandmother looked surprised.

'Goodness,' said Simon. 'It *sounds* like a foghorn.'

'It *is* Hilda,' said Mrs Tippett. 'She didn't seem too well yesterday, so we kept her in. She's going back to the field today, though.'

'Who *is* Hilda, exactly?' asked Simon.

Grandmother chuckled. 'She's rather a

friend of mine,' she said. 'She talks to me when I'm gardening. Perhaps we could go and have a word with her? I think I know where she lives.'

'You do that,' agreed Mrs Tippett, 'and I'll have your eggs ready when you come back.'

Grandmother led the way round a corner of the farmyard. Suddenly she said, 'Follow me,' and darted inside a low white building. So Simon did as well.

'Here she is,' smiled Grandmother. 'Come and say hello. She's a charming creature.'

Then Simon saw that he was inside a cowshed, and Hilda was a big, gentle look-ing cow. She had long eyelashes and twitchy ears, and she was the colour of creamy toffee. She rolled her eyes at her visitors, then raised her head and gave a loud mooing welcome.

'Hello, Foghorn Hilda,' Simon said.

Hilda clattered her feet about on the stone floor.

'Where are you going?' Grandmother called to Simon. 'She's a perfectly friendly animal.'

'I'm not going anywhere,' he said. 'I was only waiting in case you were coming.'

Hilda's face was very soft and gentle. After a while Simon went into her stall and stood beside Grandmother.

'Good old girl,' said Grandmother. She gave Hilda a slappity pat.

'Good old girl,' echoed Simon. He reached a hand up and touched Hilda's side. The cow mooed gently.

'Splendid!' said Grandmother. 'Now she's a friend of yours as well.'

Later on, when they'd said goodbye to Hilda, they both had a look round the farmyard. There didn't seem to be anyone about. Simon went inside a stable. He came out again rather quickly. 'There's a large snorting horse in there,' he said.

They met Rufus the farm dog, and discovered a litter of kittens lying in a heap of straw. They spent some time stroking the kittens.

'If I lived on a farm I'd always be patting something,' said Simon.

'Alas!' said Grandmother at last. 'It's time to go, I want to make a special pudding for lunch.'

Mrs Tippett gave them a pile of fresh eggs in a basket. At the farmyard gate Simon said, '*I'd* better take the eggs if you're going to be jumping the puddle again.'

So Grandmother obligingly leaped over three big ones, and Simon carefully squidged his way through them with the basket. When they got home they became very busy making Grandmother's special pudding.

'I'll count the eggs if you like,' Simon offered.

'Just three will do, as Great Uncle James is away,' Grandmother said.

So Simon counted out three eggs and Grandmother broke two of them into a cup. Simon broke the last one for her.

'You're not supposed to put the eggshell in as well,' said Grandmother. 'I'll butter the baking tin while you're getting it out.'

The pudding was a great success when it was finished.

'I shall rest my knees for a while on the sitting-room couch,' Grandmother said when they had washed up. 'They're not bending very well after all that jumping.'

'*I'm* not bending very well after all that pudding,' said Simon. 'I'll bring my drawing book and draw you a rather good picture.'

It was a long time later when they both heard the thumping noise coming from the kitchen.

'Heigh-ho,' said Grandmother sleepily. 'There's someone at the back door.'

'I'll go and see who it is,' said Simon.

Grandmother heard the back door open. There was an excited squeak from Simon, followed by a noisy stamping sound. As she sat up hastily, Simon dashed back, his face bright red with excitement.

'I think you'd better come!' he gasped. 'It's your friend Hilda; she's in the kitchen and she's *much* too big for it!'

'What!' Grandmother was out of the room in a moment. It was true, Hilda stood in the middle of the kitchen floor placidly nibbling a corner of the table-cloth. Her tail gently switched about around the pots and pans. She mooed in a shy way when she saw Grandmother.

'I didn't know *cows* came into your kitchen,' Simon said. He pulled the table-cloth away from Hilda.

'Nor did I,' said Grandmother, a little breathlessly.

She opened the back door wide and gave her visitor a stern look. 'Now then, Hilda, out you go.' But Hilda didn't move.

'She seems to like being here,' said Simon.

'Maybe,' said Grandmother, 'but there isn't room for all of us. The trouble is,' she added thoughtfully, 'she's too big to turn round. We'll have to push her out back-wards.'

Grandmother placed one hand on the cow's nose and the other on her shoulder. Simon decided to stay well behind and push Grandmother.

'Ready?' she said. 'Hey-up! Back, Hilda, back!'

But Hilda took a lot of pushing. First she got one bony hip wedged against the door frame, then she danced her back legs about and got the other side stuck.

'Hold hard!' Grandmother was breathing loudly. 'We'll have to think of something else.'

Hilda wagged her eyelashes and blew down Grandmother's neck.

'She seems to like you,' said Simon.

But Grandmother was thinking. 'There's only one thing to do,' she said. 'If we can't get her out backwards, she'll have to come forwards. We'll lead her through the dining-room and out of the front door.'

'Through the dining-room? Golly!' said Simon.

'Pass me that table-cloth,' ordered Grandmother.

She tied the cloth round Hilda's neck and gave it a little tug. At once the cow moved forward.

'I'll open all the doors,' said Simon.

Hilda didn't mind going through the dining-room at all. She stopped to look at some apples in a dish on the table, but one loud 'hey-up' from Grandmother got her going again. She lumbered into the hall where Simon had opened the front door as wide as it could go. Then, as they all trooped out into the front garden, Mrs Tippett appeared, running down the path.

'*There* she is,' she panted with relief. 'I'd only just put her in the field, too. Someone must have opened the gates.' Then she paused. She watched Grandmother untying the table-cloth from Hilda's neck. 'She looked as if she was coming out of your front door,' she said doubtfully.

'She *was*,' said Simon, 'and she's been in the dining-room as well. I think she came to see Grandmother.'

'I think she did,' Grandmother smiled at Mrs Tippett. 'She got a little stuck in the kitchen, you see, but she's all right now.'

'She's a very charming creature,' said Simon.

'Yes,' said Mrs Tippett, looking at them both. 'I think perhaps we'd better be off.'

As Hilda trotted gaily away to be put in the field, Simpey and Grandmother went inside.

'It was very interesting,' Simon said. 'I suppose Hilda was one of the unexpected visitors you were expecting.'

'Bless my soul!' said Grandmother, 'so she was.' She grinned at Simon. 'But I didn't think the visitor would be quite such a big one!'

Elizabeth Roberts

The Land of the Bumbley Boo

In the land of the Bumbley Boo
The people are red, white and blue,
They never blow noses
Or ever wear closes;
What a sensible thing to do!

In the land of the Bumbley Boo
You can buy Lemon Pie at the Zoo;
They give away Foxes
In little Pink Boxes
And bottles of Dandelion Stew.

In the land of the Bumbley Boo
You never see a Gnu,
But thousands of cats
Wearing trousers and hats
Made of Pumpkins and Pelican Glue!

Oh, the Bumbley Boo! the Bumbley Boo!
That's the place for me and you!
So hurry! Let's run!
The train leaves at one!
For the land of the Bumbley Boo!
The wonderful Bumbley Boo-Boo-Boo!
The wonderful Bumbley BOO!!!

Spike Milligan

Peter and Kate on the Move

For weeks Peter and Kate had been getting ready for the Move. The family was moving to a new house some distance away and everyone was excited. Even Spot the dog knew something was going to happen and followed Dad everywhere.

Peter's and Kate's father had given them a big box so that they could pack their toys and treasures themselves. So, after a lot of argument, they chose their favourite books, *Peter Rabbit* and *The Wind in the Willows* (they both liked Toad best), Lego, a 'Space attack' game, a football, Kate's 'Barbie' doll with all its sets of clothes and Peter's Dinky cars.

'I shall take my carpentry tools so that I can help Dad with the jobs in the new house,' said Peter busily.

'I can help Dad too,' said Kate. 'I like banging things with a hammer!'

When he thought nobody was looking, Peter slipped in an old felt monkey, Jacko, that he had had since he was a little boy. 'You're not going to take that old thing, are you?' protested his mother. 'Yes, I am!' said Peter. 'I couldn't just leave Jacko here, Mummy.' He tucked his old friend away in a corner of the box where no one was likely to find him and throw him away.

The trouble was that as soon as the box was packed, Peter or Kate would be sure to want something out of it – a favourite doll or a special car – so the box was always in a state of confusion. At last, when the move was only two days away, Dad said, 'Now, that's enough! I'm going to tie up your box and you mustn't open it until we are safely in the new house.'

Now the exciting day of the move had come.

'Where are you going?' asked Peter's friend, Joe, from next door.

'I don't quite know – a long way – and it's a *new* house, new bricks, a new front door and . . .'

'Are you taking your swing?'

'No – Dad says he'll make me a new one.'

'Good! Then I'll swing on it when you've gone.'

'All right – but no one else can.'

'Goodbye. I may as well have a swing *now*,' said Joe and he disappeared into Peter's garden.

'Peter!' called his mother. 'The van's here.'

Sure enough, there it was. It looked as big as a house, thought Peter, but after all everything inside the house had to be put into it. It needed to be big!

He watched as the two removers' men carried the chairs and the tables and the big wardrobe and lots of other things and loaded them into the van. The men seemed to do a lot of shouting to each other. 'This way, Jim...' 'Mind your corners...!' 'Slowly does it...' 'Told you it wouldn't go, Fred. Look what you done!'

Peter thought Fred was a very funny man! He put an easy chair over his head, carried a small chair in one hand and a frying pan in the other and hung a picture round his neck. All the time he sang and

94

whistled. Moving was fun, Peter decided.

He ran upstairs to look at his bedroom again. To his dismay Jim and Fred were knocking his bed into pieces. 'Hi!' he said indignantly, 'You're breaking up my bed!'

'Keep your hair on, young 'un,' said Jim. 'We'll put it together again when we get to the other end. If not, the floor's nice and comfortable.'

Peter was not at all sure about that.

At last the house was empty. The furniture was in the van, the carpets taken up, the curtains down. Peter's mother ran out with a last box of food and kitchen things and Daddy put in the box of plants he had grown in the greenhouse.

'Have you put in my potatoes?' asked Peter anxiously. His father had planted potatoes in the spring and Peter had planted some too.

'Sorry, Peter,' said his father. 'The potatoes aren't big enough to dig up yet and, anyway, they belong to the man who has bought our house.'

Someone else eating *his* potatoes – pounds and pounds of them! Peter didn't think that was at all fair. 'But, Dad...' he began.

'Let's go round the house and make sure nothing has been forgotten,' suggested his father hastily.

They looked into every room. It was strange to see them so empty and to hear their footsteps on the bare boards. There were light patches on the wallpaper where the pictures had hung. The house didn't feel like home anymore.

'Has anyone seen Cuddles?' asked Peter's Mum. 'I can't find her anywhere and I want to put her safely into the cat basket.'

Peter and Kate dashed about everywhere in the house, but there was nowhere to hide there now. Joe was still swinging in the garden but he said he hadn't seen Cuddles. Kate began to cry, 'Cuddles is lost – I don't want to leave Cuddles behind!'

'Would you by any chance be looking for a black cat with whiskers?' asked Fred who had been looking round the van to make sure everything was secure. 'There's one asleep on the settee here.' And there was Cuddles curled up in her usual place on the settee.

'Best leave her there,' said Peter's Dad, 'but mind she doesn't get out at the other end until we're there.'

Fred and Jim clanged the big door of the van shut and moved off slowly. 'See yer!' they shouted.

Now it was the family's turn to pack themselves into their car. Peter and Kate climbed into the back seat – Spot had jumped in already for he loved car rides and he was afraid of being left behind. Mummy pushed in a lot of oddments round the children, Daddy filled the boot with others.

'We're off!' shouted Peter and Kate. 'Goodbye, house!'

At first they looked out of the car window but it had been an exciting day and they were tired. They fell asleep and Spot slept too, his nose on Peter's foot.

When they woke they were nearly at the end of their journey. They looked out eagerly and Spot put his head out of the window, his ears flapping in the breeze.

'The first one who sees a school, *shout!*' said their father. 'Our house is in the next road to the school, on the left.'

'SCHOOL!' shouted Kate and Dad turned into a rough road. There at the end was a new-looking house with green fields beyond. And there was the furniture van parked outside and Jim and Fred were sitting on the tailboard smoking.

'Ready when you are, mate,' said Jim. Soon they were unloading the van and carrying everything into the new house. Kate ran inside with the sleepy Cuddles in her arms. Before long, the new house was full of furniture and the van was empty. After a last cup of tea, Jim and Fred drove away.

Peter and Kate rushed into the house. 'Which is my room?' Peter asked eagerly.

'I want to see *my* room,' demanded Kate.

'The big bedroom at the front is for Daddy and me,' said their mother. 'The middle-sized room at the back is Peter's because he is the oldest and the little room is Kate's because she likes to be cosy.'

They ran upstairs. Peter was anxious about his bed – would Jim and Fred have mended it properly? Yes they had and it looked as good as new. And there was their special box at the foot of the bed. The window looked out over the garden and the fields. It was a super room!

'Look at *my* room!' said Kate. It too had a window looking out over the garden. 'I *like* my room,' said Kate contentedly. 'I shall put my dolls' house just here ...'

'I'll make you some shelves with my carpentry set,' offered Peter kindly.

'I'll hammer the nails in,' said Kate.

'One quick look at the garden, children,' called their mother, 'then tea and bed. We're all tired.'

Kate was almost asleep and didn't want to go out, so Peter ran into the garden by himself, Spot barking at his heels with excitement – *he* wanted to find out what the new garden *smelt* like! The garden was big enough for Peter to play with his football and there weren't any flowerbeds to get in the way – not yet anyway. There were some thick bushes at the end, just right for playing Indians and hiding. Peter climbed the fence and looked out across the fields. What a long way he could see! There was a wood in the distance, it would be fun to explore that. He and Kate and Spot could have lots of fun together.

100

How hungry he was! He ran indoors for tea.

Later, as he snuggled down in his own bed with Jacko for company, he thought about his new home. It felt a bit strange but Mum and Dad were there and Kate and Spot and Cuddles, so everything would be all right. 'Tomorrow, Jacko,' he said sleepily, 'we'll explore and have adventures and . . .'

Peter and Kate were asleep in their new home.

Eileen Colwell

Our House

Our house is small –
The lawn and all
Can scarcely hold the flowers,
Yet every bit,
The whole of it,
Is precious, for it's ours!

From door to door,
From roof to roof,
From wall to wall we love it;
We wouldn't change
For something strange
One shabby corner of it!

The space complete
In cubic feet
From cellar floor to rafter
Just measures right,
And not too tight,
For us, and friends, and laughter.

Dorothy B. Thompson

The Big Brown Trunk

What a day it had been! Kamla's big cousin Leela had just arrived from India on a visit. The excitement had been tremendous. Earlier in the day, the whole family had gone to the airport to meet her. Even some uncles and aunts from the north had turned up. They brought garlands of yellow flowers with them to drape round Leela's neck and to welcome her in true Indian style.

When Leela had walked out of the customs hall there was a gasp of delight. No one had seen her since she was a little girl like Kamla.

Now, here was a beautiful lady, with a long black plait which fell to her waist, swishing through the doors in a glittering saree.

She was pushing a trolley with her luggage on it. There didn't seem to be very much – just one shoulder bag and one big, brown trunk with stickers all over it!

Kamla had suddenly felt shy and hung

back behind her mother as her beautiful cousin was garlanded and kissed. When Leela bent to kiss her, she was aware of a rich scent of flowers and perfume all mixed up. It made her think of India, even though she had never been there.

They had all piled into her father's car to go home. Leela's big, brown trunk was so big that Daddy couldn't shut the boot properly and had to tie it with string to keep it down.

Later, back at home, everyone had been kind and polite to Leela. They made sure that she had a nice cup of tea and they sat her down in the most comfy chair. But really, they were all dying to know what was inside Leela's big brown trunk!

At last Leela had dragged the trunk into the middle of the room. She knelt on the carpet, turned the key in the lock and lifted the lid. It was as if she had opened a treasure chest. Everyone peered into it, bursting with curiosity.

Then she had lifted up shining sarees, embroidered tunics and shirts, brightly

coloured ties and boxes of bangles. There was something for everyone. Soon the living-room was strewn with delights like a dazzling bazaar.

Leela's trunk seemed bottomless. Still she delved. She pulled out a large box of Indian sweets, and, joy of joys, a whole bag of the spices specially and lovingly ground by her grandmother. Leela handed the spices to Kamla's mother who couldn't have looked happier if she had been handed a bag of gold.

At last Leela had got up, holding a package. 'Where is Kamla?' she called. 'This is for you!'

Kamla had stepped forward, her hands tightly clasped. What had Leela brought for her?

She took the package and held it close for a moment. She always liked to try and guess what was inside a parcel before opening it. But now everyone was shouting, 'Open it! Open it! Come on, Kamla, don't keep us all in suspense!'

So Kamla had torn off the wrapping

paper quickly and everyone had sighed with pleasure at what they saw. There lay a pair of shiny satin pink pyjamas with a tunic to match.

The tunic was embroidered all down the front with tiny white beads and silver sequins which sparkled like stars. There was a long, flimsy, paler pink veil, also dotted with sequins. This was for tossing over your shoulders, or draping round your head. It was the sort of costume little Indian girls wear until they are old enough to wear sarees.

Kamla couldn't believe there was anything in the world as pretty. She put the costume on immediately. It felt shiny and cold. She paraded round the living-room while everyone admired her.

'Please can I go and show it to Kate?' she had begged.

But mother had said firmly, 'Show her tomorrow. It's past your bedtime. Say good-night!'

So Kamla had gone upstairs to bed. She had tried to sleep but she couldn't.

Downstairs everyone was eating a special rice and curry which her mother had prepared in Leela's honour. There was multicoloured pulauo rice filled with nuts and raisins and delicate spices; there was rich meat curry made with yogurt and coconut, and all sorts of smaller silver dishes filled with vegetables and pickles and mouth-watering chutneys.

Lying there on the landing, Kamla secretly watched her mother whisking to and fro from the kitchen to the dining-room. She caught glimpses of Leela as the door opened and shut. Once Leela saw her and winked, but didn't give her away.

Later, everyone went into the living-room. They flopped on the carpet around Kamla's father who got out his accordion and began to play. Leela curled up next to him. She tucked her feet inside her saree and began to sing. Someone beat a rhythm on the lid of Leela's trunk, as if it were a drum.

As her sweet voice carried its strange melodies up the stairs, Kamla's eyes at last began to feel heavy. She crept back to her room and slipped into bed. She was asleep even before she had time to pull the cover over herself.

At school the next day, Kamla couldn't stop talking about her big cousin Leela and the marvels that came out of her big brown trunk. She told the teacher and she told the dinner ladies and, of course, she told her best friend Kate.

By the end of the day, Kate was dying to see cousin Leela and this big, brown trunk which had brought such marvellous things.

'Come round and play after school,' suggested Kamla. 'Then you'll be able to see Leela.'

Leela met the girls at the door when they got home. She was pleased to meet Kate. Kamla had told her all about Kate over breakfast.

Kamla rushed upstairs. In a few moments she had torn off her grey cardigan, her grey pinafore dress and her school socks and shoes. She came slowly downstairs like a queen, wearing her new shiny pink satin pyjamas and tunic, with the veil tossed loosely round her shoulders.

Kate gazed in amazement.

'Did that come out of the big brown trunk?' she cried. Then she walked round and round her friend, fingering the delicate veil and smoothing her hand over the cool satin.

Then Kate whispered to Kamla that she wanted to see the big brown trunk.

'It's upstairs,' whispered Kamla.

The two girls bounded upstairs and rushed into Leela's room. 'It's under the bed,' cried Kamla. So they flopped down on the floor on their tummies and peered under the counterpane.

'It's very big,' whispered Kate. 'Is it empty now?'

'I'm not sure,' replied Kamla.

'What are you two up to?' exclaimed Leela, coming in.

'I was showing Kate your big brown trunk,' cried Kamla, jumping up. 'I told her it was full of wonderful things, like a treasure chest. I told her that my tunic and pyjamas had come out of it. Have you got any pyjamas for Kate?'

Leela got down on her knees and pulled the trunk out from under the bed.

'Are you going to open it?' asked Kate excitedly.

'This treasure chest, as you call it, may have something in it for you, though not pyjamas, I'm afraid,' said Leela.

Kate watched, hardly daring to breathe, as the catches flew open and Leela lifted the lid. She rummaged round for a few moments among her sarees and blouses, and then said, 'Ah! This is what I was looking for!'

She got up holding a shining white veil, shot with silver threads which sparkled in the sunlight.

'Can I keep it?' squeaked Kate. She could hardly believe her eyes.

'Yes,' said Leela, smiling. 'Because you're Kamla's best friend.'

Kamla helped her to toss the glittering

veil round her shoulders. 'All you need now are the tunic and pyjamas, and then you'll look really Indian!'

'I've got pyjamas! I'll go and put them on!' and Kate dashed off home leaving Kamla and Leela looking puzzled.

After a while she came back. Kamla and Leela clapped their hands with delight.

There stood Kate in her own pink flannelette pyjamas! She didn't seem to mind that

the pyjama top had little blue engines chugging all over it. Across her shoulders she had tossed the beautiful white and silver veil which Leela had give her.

'There you are!' cried Kate proudly. 'Now I look Indian!'

'You look lovely!' exclaimed Leela.

'Thank you very much for the veil,' said Kate. 'It's the most beautiful thing I've ever had.'

'I told you that Leela's big brown trunk was a treasure chest,' laughed Kamla.

'Let's go downstairs now,' said Leela, pushing the big brown trunk back under the bed. 'I've been making all sorts of nice goodies for tea.'

Jamila Gavin

Jenny

Her aunties trains of satin don
    When going to a ball –
But Jenny puts the bath-towel on
    And trails it down the hall.

There's diamonds on her mother's gown,
    And rubies in her hair –
But Jenny has a cake-tin crown
    And curtain-rings to wear.

Her sister at the dance prefers
    Some other lady's dress –
But Jenny's satisfied with hers,
    For *she*'s a *real* Princess!

Eleanor Farjeon

A Little Help from Jane

When Jane woke up on Christmas morning, she knew right away that something *special* was going to happen. Today she would get her bike! Jane wanted a bike more than anything else in the world. Her older brother Harry had a bike, a bright red one with blue wheels and high handlebars, and so did Sharon next door. Even Peter across the road, who was the same age as Jane, had a bike of his own. But whenever Jane asked her mother and father if *she* could have a bicycle too, they said that she wasn't old enough yet and, besides, they couldn't afford it.

But Jane *knew* that she would get a bike this Christmas. She felt so sure of it that she didn't get up right away. She lay in bed with her eyes closed, listening to the silence of the house and trying to stop her stomach wobbling with excitement. Her mother had told her that this feeling was called 'having butterflies' but it didn't feel like butterflies at all – it was much, much more than that, like lots of excitement and laughter all bunched up, waiting to come bursting out. Jane knew that this was the day when she would get her bike at last; she pressed her eyes shut and pictured the bicycle waiting for her in her room, a luggage label dangling from the handlebars reading, 'To Jane, with love from Mummy and Daddy'.

Slowly Jane opened her eyes. Her bedroom was still quite dark but there was enough light in the sky outside for her to make out the shape of the furniture in her room. She looked round carefully but she could see nothing that was new. Then she sat up in bed to get a better look and her stomach gave a great lurch when she saw a large white pillowcase at the foot of the bed. Her presents!

Jane dragged the pillowcase towards her. It bulged in an interesting way and felt hard and crackly. It smelled faintly of oranges too, because there were fruit and nuts inside as well as presents. The pillowcase was too small to hold a bicycle, though, so Jane looked anxiously round the room for it. But even in the half light she could see that there was no bike there.

Just for a moment, Jane felt as though she was going to cry but then she had a sudden thought. The bike was too big to be in her bedroom! Her father would have left it downstairs, propped up against the umbrella stand in the hall! Jane jumped out of bed and ran on to the landing. Hardly daring to breathe, she peered through the banisters into the hall below. And then her heart sank. There was no bike there. No bike at all. Sadly, she went back to bed and waited for the day to begin.

Jane enjoyed the rest of Christmas Day; she enjoyed opening her presents and she enjoyed helping her parents and her brother to open theirs. And then there was the special dinner, with turkey and Christmas pudding. After that, in the afternoon, Jane's grandad came to tea. Grandad was the person Jane loved best in all the world, after her parents. He was quite old and his head was bald, except for a fringe of white hair round the edge. But his eyes twinkled all the time and he was always ready to have an adventure with Jane. Grandad knew all about animals and plants, and how to grow trees from apple pips. He spent much of his time growing vegetables and flowers on his allotment and Jane liked nothing better than to help him weed and water them. Sometimes, on summer evenings, Grandad would take Jane home on his old bike. 'Let's go for a spin, young Jane,' he would say. 'And we'll take some dahlias home to your mother.' The old man had made a special wooden seat for Jane that was fixed to the crossbar of his bike, and off the two of them would ride, the bunch of flowers tied to the handlebars, and Jane ringing the bicycle bell for all she was worth.

Now, on Christmas afternoon, Jane decided to tell Grandad all about the bike that she wanted so badly. Grandad listened to her carefully with a serious expression on his face. Then, when Jane had told him everything, the old man said, 'Well, young

118

Jane, if you want a bike we'll have to make one!'

Jane laughed. Her grandad was always cracking jokes. 'You can't do that,' she said. 'You can only get bikes from a special shop. I've seen them.'

Grandad looked thoughtful. 'I suppose you want one of those shiny modern ones that Harry and his friends have got?'

Jane nodded. She'd watched Harry and the other boys and girls doing wheelies and bunny hops and tabletops with their BMX bikes. She knew exactly the kind of bicycle she wanted.

'Can't be done, girl,' Grandad said. 'Much too expensive.' Then he grinned. 'I'll *make* you a bike, if you want. I'll make you a bike that will be different from all the others, a bike that will be a treat to ride.'

Jane smiled and said thank you but inside she didn't feel too sure. She didn't really want a bike that was different from the others; she wanted a bike that was just the same. A proper bike like those Harry and Sharon and Peter had. She hoped that Grandad would forget all about it.

But Grandad didn't forget. A few days later he came to Jane's home. He had an old bicycle frame with him. 'Look, girl!' he cried. 'I found this at the scrap metal yard. They gave it to me free because there aren't any wheels. We'll use it for *your* bike!'

When Grandad had gone, Jane sat and stared miserably at the frame. It was old and the black paint was chipped. It looked nothing at all like the gleaming red frame of Harry's bike or Sharon's yellow one. And then a strange thing happened. As Jane stared at the chipped and rusty frame, she remembered how happy her grandad had been because he had found the first part of Jane's bike. And, as she remembered Grandad's happiness, she realized that the old man was right, after all. A bike made specially for her *would* be better than an ordinary shop bike. It would be the only one of its kind in the world.

The next day was Saturday and Grandad

arrived on his bike first thing in the morning. He had a bag of sandwiches with him, and a flask of tea. 'Come on, Jane,' he said. 'We're off to visit Aladdin's Cave to look for the rest of your bike.'

'What's Aladdin's Cave?' Jane asked.

'It's the big scrap metal yard in town,' Grandad said. 'It'll be hard work so I've brought some sandwiches in case we get hungry.'

Aladdin's Cave was a huge yard surrounded by a high wire fence. It was guarded by a large fierce-looking dog. The yard was piled high with so much scrap metal that Jane didn't know where to look first. There were old cars with smashed windows and crumpled doors, broken washing machines, old cookers and battered metal sheds. To one side of the yard stood a huge crane which picked up the old cars as if they were made of paper and dropped them into a machine that crushed and squashed them into small blocks of metal. In another part of the yard, men were sorting through old freezers and metal cupboards, knocking the doors off with big hammers as they laughed and joked with each other.

Grandad spoke to the man in charge of the yard, who pointed to a corner far away from the noise of the crushing machine and the men with hammers. Grandad beckoned to Jane and together they walked up to the heap of metal which lay there. This was what they had come to see; a mountain of metal bits and pieces that no one else wanted. If they were lucky, they might find some bicycle wheels and handlebars to go with the frame that Grandad had already found.

It took Jane and her grandad all day to

search through the heap of metal, but, by teatime, they had found just what they wanted: a saddle, two wheels that weren't twisted, and a pair of handlebars that were almost as good as new.

During the next few days, Grandad worked very hard on the bike and Jane helped him when she came home from school. First, the old frame had to be rubbed down and painted bright blue. Jane helped with the painting, though she managed to get more paint on herself than she did on the frame. Then the wheels were checked to make sure that the spokes were straight and the rim was sound. Grandad bought two new tyres, brake blocks, brake pads and a pump, and he showed Jane how to fit them. After the wheels had been put into the frame, the pedals and chain were cleaned and oiled and then fitted to the frame and back wheel.

The bike was beginning to take shape now. It looked a little old-fashioned but Jane didn't care. She thought that the big wheels would make the bike go much faster than smaller modern ones. The handlebars were cleaned and fitted next, and then the saddle was put in place.

Jane and Grandad gazed proudly at the bicycle. It was finished at last. Or was it?

'There's something missing,' Grandad muttered. 'Ah, I know! Mudguards! We must have those, they finish a bike off!'

Next day, in a nearby junk shop, they found just what they needed: two bright red mudguards. 'They'll make the bike stand out from the others,' Grandad said cheerfully. And then, as a finishing touch, Jane bought a gleaming silver bell with her pocket money. Harry and Sharon and Peter had horns on their bikes but she wanted a bell like her grandad's.

At last Jane's bike really was finished. The fresh paint shone and the new silver bell glittered in the winter sunlight. The bright colours couldn't hide the fact that the bike looked old-fashioned or that the saddle was made of hard leather instead of being soft and padded like those on modern bikes. But Jane had never in her life seen a more beautiful machine. It was the only one of its kind in the whole world. Her grandad had made it specially for her, and she had helped.

'Well, come on, Jane,' her grandad said. 'Aren't you going to ride it?'

Jane wheeled the bike out of the garden gate and on to the quiet road beyond. As if in a dream, she sat down, grasping the handlebars in front of her. Slowly she lifted her foot on to a pedal and pushed off. She could feel her grandad's hand on the saddle behind her helping to keep the bike steady. At first the bike wobbled around but then Jane got her balance and the bike slowly gathered speed.

Jane laughed out loud with happiness, and rang the bell as loudly as she could. She wanted everyone in the world to see her new bike, the very special bike that her grandad had made – with a little help from Jane, of course.

Lance Salway

The Bulldozer

An orange-coated man
Who wears for his work
The colour of coat
You see in the dark
Starts the engine
Bang-b-bang-bang.

The bulldozer scoop
Is like a boot
As if a giant
Smoothed the ground
With the sole of his foot
Down-d-down-down.

Digging its tracks
Into the mud
The yellow bulldozer
Bends its back
Like a butting bull
Charge-ch-charge-thud.

It lifts loose earth
Away from its feet
And drops it in a heap
Or dumps it in a truck.
Bump-b-bump-full.

Stanley Cook

The Little Fir-Tree

It was a few days before Christmas. The children looked through their windows and shouted gleefully: 'It's snowing! Look! Snow for Christmas!' and they jumped for joy.

'I told you so,' said their mother. 'I said it would snow!'

'Tomorrow we'll play snowballs, and ride in the sledge and make a snowman,' cried the children excitedly, as they went to bed.

Soon the earth was white, covered with the fine feathery mantle thrown down from the sky. The grass and the trees felt warm under the snow. In the wood every dark branch was outlined with silver, and every holly leaf held a bunch of snowflakes in its hollowed green cup. The great branches spread out their bare boughs and caught the snow in their nest of twigs, and the birches stood like frozen fountains, very beautiful.

Near the edge of the wood was a plantation of fir-trees, all very young and small.

Their dark outstretched skirts were soon white, so that each tree looked like a little shining umbrella. Now one tree was different from the others, for it possessed a treasure which it held tightly to its heart. It was a nest, which had been built in the spring by a speckled thrush. It was so neat and trim that the fir-tree was very proud of it, and sheltered it with its close thick branches so that no snow fell into it.

The little fir-tree had loved the singing bird which lived there. It had taken care of the eggs and guarded the nestlings from owls and robbers until they were old enough to fly away. It had listened to the thrush's song and moved its slender branches to the music. When the birds went, the tree waited for them to return or for another bird to come to the empty nest, but the rain fell and the winds blew, and no bird sat in the home hidden in the heart of the tree.

'Perhaps a winter bird will come, a dazzling white bird, and it will lay eggs of ivory and pearl in my nest,' said the little fir-tree when it saw the snow, but the other trees round it shook their heads till the snow fell in a shower.

'Only hens could do that,' said they, 'and they stay in the farmyards this wintry weather. There will be no bird till next year.'

Then they drooped their branches and waited patiently till they were completely covered up again by the warm white blanket.

In a cottage down the lane lived a little boy and girl. They made a fine snowman outside their kitchen window, and stuck an old broken pipe of their grandfather's in its wide mouth, and a stick in its hand. They pulled each other up and down in a wooden box, pretending it was a sledge drawn by a pair of fine horses. They made a long slide in the lane, and glided along it, with arms outstretched to the cold air, pretending they were flying birds. They looked at the icy frost ferns on the windows of the little rooms under the thatched roof, and called them 'Jack Frost's Garden'.

130

'The children in the castle are going to have a Christmas tree,' proclaimed Peter, pushing his wet red hand into his mother's.

'And it's going to be all a-dazzle with lights and things,' said Sarah.

'Such things are not for us. They cost too much money, but you are going to have a pair of boots apiece, and that's more useful. Maybe Santa Claus will put something in your stocking, too, if you're good.' Their mother sighed, knowing how hard it was to manage. She packed them off early to bed, but the grandfather nodded his head and smiled to himself.

On Christmas Eve, the old man came into the wood, carrying a spade. He hunted here and there looking at this tree and that, peering at the colony of firs like a wise owl that wants to find a home. One tree was too big, another too scraggy, another too bushy. Then he saw the little fir-tree, standing like a fairy on one leg, wearing a crinoline of snowy crystals.

'That's the tree! That's the tree for me! Not too big, and not too little, with plenty of close branches, as smooth and round as a ball,' he cried aloud, for like many old people he had a habit of speaking to himself for company.

He shook the snow from the twigs with tender fingers and then dug round the tree, gathering all the fibrous roots carefully in his hand.

'Oh dear me!' cried the little fir-tree. 'What is going to happen? Don't shake the nest out of my branches!' The sound of its voice was like a sobbing breeze, and the other trees shook their heads and waved their tiny boughs mournfully.

'Goodbye,' they called. 'Goodbye for ever.'

'Whatever happens, I am glad. It's a great adventure,' the little fir-tree sang out bravely, when the old man carried it away.

Across the fields and along the lane it went in the grandfather's warm hands, and the tall trees in the hedgerows looked with pity at it. Little rabbits peeped round the corners of the walls, and a hare stared through a gap to see who was singing the song of the woods. When they saw the

132

fir-tree they nodded and whispered: 'Poor thing! He's caught in a trap!' and they scurried away.

The grandfather walked through a wooden gate, and up the path to the cottage door. Then he put the tree in the woodshed till the children went to bed. He wiped his spade, washed his hands and sat down to tea without saying anything.

At last it was bedtime, and Peter and Sarah had their baths on the kitchen hearth, where a great fire blazed, and sparks flew up the chimney. They sat on their stools and ate their bread and milk, and a mince pie because it was Christmas Eve. Then they each took a candle and trundled up the crooked stair to their little beds, but just as they kissed good night to their mother and grandfather, Peter lifted his head and listened.

'I can hear a little singing noise,' said he. 'What is it?'

Sarah listened too. 'It's only the wind in the woodshed,' she told her brother, and she ran to tie her stocking to the bedpost, ready for Santa Claus.

When all was quiet upstairs, the grandfather fetched the little tree into the house. The fire crackled, and the tree began to tremble with the heat, so that the twigs

134

rustled and its song died away in fright. 'This is the end,' it thought.

'Here's a little tiddly Christmas tree for Peter and Sarah,' said the old man. 'But take great care of it, for I must put it back in the wood where I found it.'

The mother dropped her sewing and smiled at her father. 'Oh, Grandfather! What a surprise! What a perfect little tree!'

She gazed at the green tree, with its shining branches to which a powder of snow still clung. There was something particularly beautiful about this tree, fresh from its dreams in the forest. As for the little fir-tree, it plucked up its courage and stared round the room, at the table with the bread and cheese, and the cat on the hearth, and the china dogs on the mantelpiece, and the holly wreath over the loud ticking clock.

'There's a nest in it,' went on the grandfather proudly, 'Peter will like that,' and he showed the mother the neat round nest hidden under the branches.

'Now I'm going out to buy some things to hang on it, so that it will be as fine as the tree up at the castle. You plant it carefully all ready for me!' He reached up to the teapot on the mantelpiece, the lustre teapot which was his money-box, and took out some coins.

'I'm going to be extravagant for once, for I've got a bit of my pension left,' he laughed, and he set off down the dark lanes to the village shop.

While he was away, the mother planted the tree in plenty of soil in the big earthenware breadmug which stood in the corner of the room, stocked with her home-made loaves. The bread she placed in a row on the dresser, small round cobs each with a cross on the top in memory of the Christ Child, and the tree she dragged to the middle of the room, near the lamp and her sewing. As her needle went in and out she heard a tiny singing sound, and she knew it was the happy tree chanting its woodland song.

After some time the old man came back with a brown-paper parcel and bulging pockets. From the parcel he took little red and blue and gold balls to hang on the tree, and a silver glass trumpet, and four tiny coloured glass bells with little clappers which tinkled like icicles. He had a box of silver tassels to droop from the boughs like falling water, and a couple of gold roses. He brought from his pocket two oranges, and three rosy apples, and a couple of baskets of almond fruits. The mother and the old man hung them all about the tree, so that it looked as if the little glossy fir-tree had stepped straight out of fairyland.

On the tip-top of the tree's head, the grandfather's shaking fingers fastened a little Dutch doll with a wisp of tinsel round her waist, a midget of a doll as big as his thumb-nail, and in the nest he placed a lovely little glass bird, with a white body and feathery tail and a silver beak and wings.

The tree quivered with delight so that all the bells began to ring, and all the balls and sparkles jumped up and down and gleamed in the firelight. At last a bird had come to live in the nest again, a winter bird, snow-white like the frosty earth!

138

Throughout the Christmas Eve the tree stayed in the quiet room, listening to the ticking of the clock, and the chink, chink of the dying fire, and the chirrup of the cricket which lived under the hearthstone, and the tree, too, murmured and rustled its branches, waiting for the glass bird to chirp and sing.

Then dawn came, and the mother made the fire again, so that the lights sprang out and the tree's dark branches reflected the glow. The kettle sang, the blue cups and saucers were placed with their tinkling spoons on the clean white cloth, and the bacon hissed in the frying-pan.

Suddenly there was a patter of feet, and a sound of laughter on the stairs. The door burst open and the two children came running in, carrying bulging little stockings in their hands.

'A Merry Christmas! A Merry Christmas!' they cried, hugging their mother and grandfather. Then they saw the pretty tree standing as demure as a little girl in her first party frock, and they gave a shout.

139

'A Christmas tree! Where did it come from? Oh, how lovely! It's a real live one, growing.'

'There's a teeny, tiny doll on the top. Is it for me?' asked Sarah.

'There's a real nest,' exclaimed Peter, 'and there's a bird in it too.' They both danced round the tree singing:

'Christmas comes but once a year,
And when it comes it brings good cheer.'

'Just see if that bird has laid any eggs,' said the smiling old grandfather, and when Peter slipped his hand in the thrush's nest he found two silver sixpences!

That was a day for the fir-tree to remember. Never as long as it lived would it forget that day! It stood, the centre of the festivities, watching the Christmas games, listening to the Christmas songs, humming softly to the bells from the church across the village green.

'Can't you hear it?' whispered Peter. 'The tree is singing.' But Sarah said it was only the wind through the keyhole, for trees never sang.

In a few days the grandfather took the fir-tree back to the wood, with the nest safe and sound under its branches. He uncovered the hole, and planted the roots deep in it, so that the tree stood firmly amongst its companions.

'Tell us again,' cried the fir-trees in the plantation, when the little tree had told its story for the hundredth time. 'Did you say a snow-white bird came to live in your nest? Did you have bells on your boughs? And gold roses? Tell us again.'

So once more the fir-tree told the story of Christmas.

'But the bird never sang at all,' it added. 'I shall be glad to see my thrush again next spring. The bells were not as sweet-sounding as the bluebells in the wood, and the roses had no scent at all. But it was a beautiful Christmas, and I was very, very happy!'

Alison Uttley

142

For Christmas

Now not a window small or big
But wears a wreath of holly sprig;
Nor any shop too poor to show
Its spray of pine or mistletoe.
Now city airs are spicy-sweet
With Christmas trees along each street,
Green spruce and fir whose boughs still
    hold
Their tinsel balls and fruits of gold.
Now postmen pass in threes or fours
Like bent, blue-coated Santa Claus.
Now people hurry to and fro
With little girls and boys in tow,
And not a child but keeps some trace
Of Christmas secrets in his face.

Rachel Field

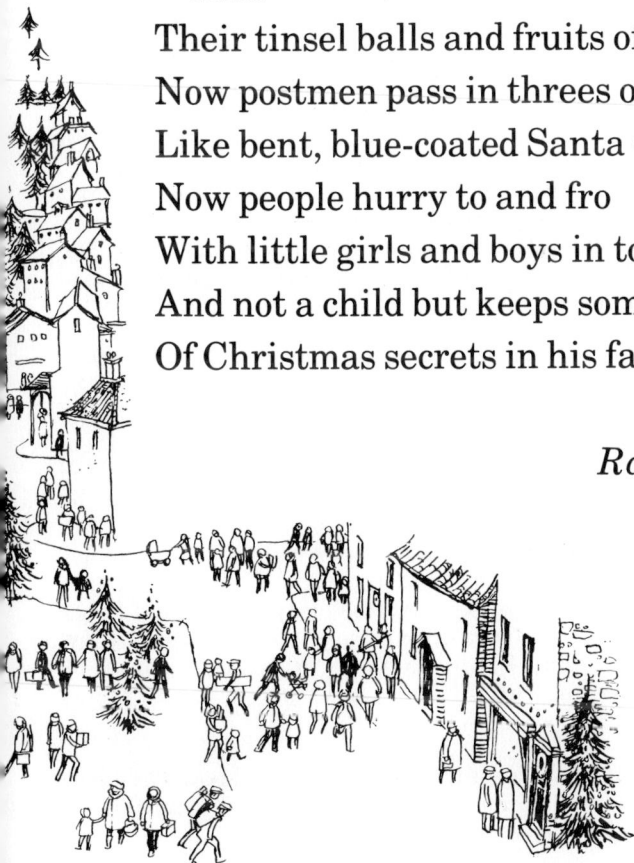

Acknowledgements

The editor and publishers gratefully acknowledge permission to reproduce copyright material in this anthology:

'Sea' from *Stranger than Unicorns* by Leonard Clark, reprinted by permission of Dobson Books Limited; 'The Picnic Basket' from the book *The Poppy Seed Cakes* by Margery Clark copyright © 1924 by Bantam, Doubleday, Dell Publishing Group Inc., reprinted by permission of The Bodley Head and Doubleday; 'Peter and Kate on the Move' copyright © Eileen Colwell, 1988; 'To See the Queen' copyright © Eileen Colwell, 1988; 'J for John' by Vera Colwell from *The Youngest Storybook* edited by Eileen Colwell, reprinted by permission of The Bodley Head; 'The Bulldozer' copyright © Stanley Cook, 1988; 'Jenny' from *The Children's Bells* by Eleanor Farjeon published by Oxford University Press, reprinted by permission of David Higham Associates Limited; 'For Christmas' from *The Pointed People* by Rachel Field copyright 1924, 1930, reprinted with permission of Macmillan Publishing Company from *Poems* by Rachel Field (New York: Macmillan 1957); 'The New Baby' copyright © Judith Garratt, 1988; 'The Big Brown Trunk' from *Kamla and Kate* by Jamila Gavin, reprinted by permission of Methuen Children's Books; 'The Friendly Cinnamon Bun' from *The Pedalling Man* by Russell Hoban, reprinted by permission of William Heinemann Limited and David Higham Associates Limited; 'My Brother' from *That Was Summer* by Marci Ridlon McGill, first published by Follett Publishing Co., N.Y., 1969; 'The Land of the Bumbley Boo' by Spike Milligan, reprinted by permission of the author; 'The Hippopotamus's Birthday' from *The Flattered Flying Fish and Other Poems* by E.V. Rieu, reprinted by permission of Methuen & Co. Ltd; 'An Unexpected Visitor' from *All About Simon and His Grandmother* by Elizabeth Roberts, reprinted by permission of Methuen Children's Books; 'Luke's Exciting Day' copyright © Anne Rooke, 1988; 'A Little Help from Jane' copyright © 1988 by Lance Salway; 'The Little Fir-Tree' reprinted by permission of Faber and Faber Ltd, from *Mustard, Pepper and Salt* by Alison Uttley; 'A Friend For Danny' by Ursula Moray Williams, reprinted by kind permission of Curtis Brown, copyright © Ursula Moray Williams, 1988.

Every effort has been made to trace copyright holders. The editor and publishers would like to hear from any copyright holders not acknowledged.